REVENGE OF THE SPORTS WIDOWS

REVENGE OF THE SPORTS WIDOWS:

HOW TO COPE WITH A SPORTS FANATIC

KATHLEEN BRIDGE BARRY

S.p.i.
BOOKS

S.P.I. BOOKS
A division of Shapolsky Publishers, Inc.

For any additional information, contact:
S.P.I. BOOKS
136 West 22nd Street, New York, NY 10011

Tel. (212) 633-2022
Fax (212) 633-2123

ISBN 1-56171-063-6

First Edition 1993

1 2 3 4 5 6 7 8 9 10

Manufactured in the United States of America

DEDICATION

This explorative study of the male species should allow all of womanhood worldwide to exorcise our demons and hopefully shed a little light on what can be done to cope with the self-centered, abusive, "Sports Fanatics" in our lives.

This book is dedicated to my husband Marc, who is my primary source of inspiration for this book. His sports fanaticism and comedic wit make our marriage more than interesting. And to my Dad, Ron Bridge, the ultimate sports fanatic, who is up in heaven right now rooting for the Angels.

Last but not least, this is dedicated to all of the sports "widows," who, along with me, search for the one day when our men arise from their self-imposed spiritual graves and once again join the living!

CONTENTS

INTRODUCTION

As I write this introduction, I am watching the Knicks play the Bulls in the NBA play-offs. I have taped the game, because earlier we went out to celebrate Mother's Day and our sixth wedding anniversary. At the restaurant, I implored all the waiters and the people at the next table not to talk about the outcome of the game, as I would be watching it later. I even intimated to the head waiter that it would mean a reduction in his tip if anyone on his staff blew it. On the way home, I would not allow my wife to play the radio, for fear of accidentally hearing the score. I told her if we see any neighbors standing outside, to just speed by them and we'll explain it tomorrow. When we got home, she tried to lure me into the bedroom for an anniversary *rendez vous*, but I said, "Maybe after the play-offs."

The phone has rung three times while I'm writing this, but I'll get back to all of them. Because I'm watching the Bulls play the Knicks right now and there's nothing else important in the world: not my wife, my kids, sex or money (well, it depends on how much).

Introduction

This is the living hell my wife goes through almost every day. Why did she marry me? Because she had no idea. All of us sports fanatics keep it well hidden during the courting process. It begins to surface during the engagement period and finally rears its ugly head during the honeymoon, sometimes on the very first night.

So read the horrible story now and learn about the warning signs before you become a guest on Geraldo or Oprah. Maybe for some of you it's too late, but then again, maybe not!

Yours truly,
Marc Barry, S.F.

P.S. The Knicks are winning!

CHRONOLOGY

I have often wondered where the obsession with sports began. I guess it can be traced back to one of the oldest written histories of humankind, The Bible. Yes, the Bible actually starts off with that old baseball adage, "In the big inning!" Could it be that Adam was so bored with Eve that

he took to tossing apples as far as he could, setting the stage for the evolution of modern day quarterbacks and pitchers? Maybe Eve just wasn't enticing enough to keep old Adam happy? Or could it be that once those leaves came off, Eve didn't give a "fig" for Adam and decided to take up with the snake?

EVENT	WHAT IT LED TO
Cavemen choosing mates	Baseball bats
David and Goliath	Need for team physicians
Samson and Delilah	Women team owners
Christians vs. the Lions	Giving odds
Roman orgies	Sports figures promoting "Slimfast"
Knights in armor	Jock straps & cups
Ben Franklin flying a kite	Stadium lights for night games
Paul Revere's famous ride	Horse racing handicaps
The Civil War	American vs. the National League
Women burning bras	Bouncing cheerleaders
The bombing of Pearl Harbor	The Sony Watchman
Formation of labor unions	Million dollar sports contracts
The invention of television	Sunday Night Football Monday Night Football The Thursday night edition of Monday Night Football
Evening sports on television	Test tube babies

"Sports-aholism—A crippling anti-social disease that affects three out of every four males."

AN EARLY VICTIM OF SPORTS ABUSE

While deepset feelings of shame and guilt prevent more women from coming forward and reporting on their fathers, boyfriends and brothers, there are more than ten million reported cases of sports abuse in this country every year. This is my story.

Being the only girl in my family I was unmercifully subjected to gross negligence, mental cruelty and other kinds of sports abuse by my father and brothers. For some reason (related to my gender, of course) I wasn't included in the Fraternal Athletes Rooting Team (F.A.R.T.). On Sunday afternoons my loneliness would drive me to the closed door of the room from which all the sounds of raucous pleasure and pain were emanating. Waiting for the next beer commercial, before daring to approach, I would meekly knock on the forbidden door.

"Who the hell is there?" came the predictably gruff reply.

"Kathy" I mumbled softly, "can I come in?"

"No way. What's the secret password?"

Should I have demanded equal rights? How could I? Until I turned twenty-one I always thought E.R.A. stood for Earned Run Average! Well years later I finally asked my father, "By the way, what was that secret password?"

"Male" he smugly answered. I should have known!

I remember how in my early years at home even my Barbie doll never saw her "big guy" Ken. That macho man was always in the "Dreamhouse" den watching sports on his half-inch screen. I remember putting Barbie in a sheer, sexy see-through negligee and having her prance around in front of Ken and his drinking buddy Allen. Funny, they never even blinked! Believe me when I tell you that in those days Barbie was ready, willing and able—but those jerks were too

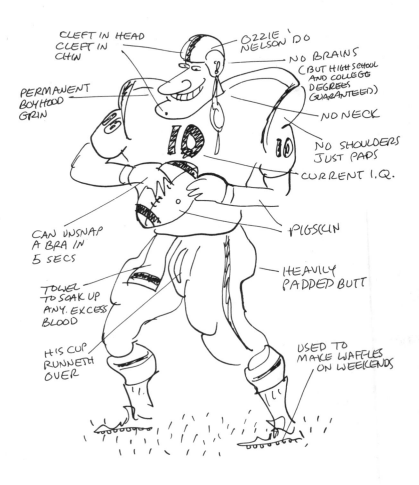

CLEFT IN HEAD
CLEFT IN CHIN

OZZIE NELSON 'DO

NO BRAINS
(BUT HIGH SCHOOL AND COLLEGE DEGREES GUARANTEED)

PERMANENT BOYHOOD GRIN

NO NECK

NO SHOULDERS JUST PADS

CURRENT I.Q.

CAN UNSNAP A BRA IN 5 SECS

PIGSKIN

TOWEL TO SOAK UP ANY. EXCESS BLOOD

HEAVILY PADDED BUTT

HIS CUP RUNNETH OVER

USED TO MAKE WAFFLES ON WEEKENDS

into their game to recognize a major opportunity and to take advantage of it.

When I turned thirteen I decided to become a tomboy so that I could finally get some attention from the opposite sex. If I was lucky enough, they would occasionally let me carry the jug of Gatorade or I could be the team nurse. The few times the guys did let me play football, I'm sure those cretins purposely threw the ball so it slammed right into my chest area causing me lots of embarrassment and pain as it would ricochet off my developing — let's call them muscles — and I would turn red-faced with shame. The result of this abuse is that I'm considering breast augmentation surgery to offset the damage those buffoons caused.

In high school, football games were places to get away from parents, get felt-up, drink vodka and orange juice and then get really sick behind the bleachers. I was even lucky enough to go out with the captain of the football team, a genuine B.M.O.C. (Big Man on Campus). Intellectually, he was about as stimulating as watching corn grow. (I'm from the Midwest—so what about it!) He was one of those big talking, smooth conversationalists when surrounded by his adoring buddies—but when left alone with an intelligent, over-sexed woman such as myself, this macho-jock was suddenly all fumbles and couldn't get to first base without my showing him the way! We're talking major, big time, all talk and no action!

In those simpler days I really didn't mind that the same air they used to pump up the football was used to fill the space between his ears (I was naive and foolishly impressed with his act), because he was the Captain of the team, which in turn transformed me into the school's hot little Homecoming Queen! Why are high school girls so attracted to these male versions of the blonde bombshell? It definitely wasn't because of all the attention they paid us! Unfortunately, in looking back I have to conclude that we were behaving like ignorant social climbers to be so attracted to such self-centered, pompous, uncaring, anti-intellectual, empty, simple, show-offs. My brother spent more time than I did with my boyfriend, watching games, comparing stats and critiquing the cheerleaders assets.

The only quality time I can remember with guys, growing up, was at the neighborhood drive-in where I had to occasionally fight off their budding adolescent hormones. Thank God boys at this age have more than sports on their minds—the only problem is that men peak at eighteen and women when they're thirty! (The age when most men are brain dead from too many radioactive rays from sports viewing on the television!)

I met my husband in New York City, the cultural mecca of the world. At first, he wined and dined me; we went to Off-Broadway plays, the ballet and concerts in Central Park. We discussed such "heavy" things as neo-existentialism, the influence of Japanese imports on the Merchandise Trade Deficit, where the dollar and the price of gold were headed, and other weighty, highbrow subjects! Rarely was the dreaded "sports" word mentioned. I thought, this is the man for me!

I should have had a clue about what was in store for me, when at a party a friend asked my fiancé when we had first met.

Incredibly, he blurted out, "September 16th, the day the Broncs beat the Falcs."

Because my job entailed a lot of traveling , I didn't really have any time to deal with all of the important decisions that go into planning and preparing a special wedding. So I left

6

it up to my fiancé to handle all of the wedding decisions. Boy, were we all in for a big surprise!

During our wedding ceremony the Justice of the Peace kept whispering these strange numbers in between the wedding vows: "Do you, Marc, take Kathy (The Jets over the Vikings by 3), to be your lawfully wedded wife ..." And that was only the tip of the iceberg!

The pain and embarrassment of reliving the whole experience is almost too disgusting to relate, but for the wedding reception, my loving man told me the color theme he picked out was green and white. I didn't see any problem with that and I thought it would actually be rather serene and country-like. On the day of the wedding when I walked into the hotel's grand ballroom and saw the kind of green and white he had in mind. I immediately assumed we were on "Totally Hidden Video," because no real wedding could be set up like this was. To begin with, instead of conventional place settings, each table was draped in astro turf and arranged together in the configuration of a baseball diamond! Instead of having place cards, we had custom made score cards that stated "The Johnsons—3rd Base," "The Simpsons—Center Field," etc. And of course my thoughtful fiancé planned the bridal dais at "home plate." As bad as this all seems, it managed to get worse. Before dinner was served we had to stand for the national anthem. His buddies loved it; my family all wanted to walk out. We stayed because we remembered that we were picking up the bill for my new husband's insanity. Besides, our family lawyer was at the wedding and counseled that I now had sound, irrefutable grounds for divorce, any time I wanted. This made Daddy a little happier and we decided to spend the rest of the wedding with the film crew to be sure they got all the evidence on videotape.

DATING AND THE SPORTS FANATIC

Your dream date, a man for all seasons

There are some of us out there who are just starting out in the dating scene. It's important to find out before you become romantically involved with a sports fanatic to what degree you really hate sports. Below is a multiple choice test designed to determine whether you should date a sports fanatic or drop him as soon as you meet him!

HOW MUCH DO YOU HATE SPORTS?

1. When you were young and you were trying to get your father's attention you would:

   A.) Jump up onto his lap and snuggle while he watches TV.
   B.) Go to the bookstore and read up on all his favorite teams.
   C.) Wear slutty clothes, hang around with druggies and have a tattoo that says "I'm Easy" emblazoned on your chest.

2. Growing up did you:

   A.) Play softball with all the neighborhood boys.
   B.) Excel in field hockey during gym class.
   C.) Tell everyone that you had mononucleosis and that your doctor said the only exercise you could safely handle was turning the pages of "Harlequin" romance books.

3. How important a part of your life is sports:

   A.) Without sports your world would be boring and meaningless.
   B.) You have your own mitt to bring to baseball games that even your little nephew isn't allowed to borrow.

C.) Watching sports is synonymous with having PMS, a face full of acne and a hundred hours of pushing during hard labor.

4. When given the choice of attending the final game of the World Series or having a lobotomy, you would:

    A.) Spend six hundred dollars just to fly to the game.
    B.) Disguise yourself as the San Diego chicken just to get in.
    C.) Uurgh uug eeaagh

5. When your man says he'd rather watch the hockey game than go to your acceptance banquet for the Nobel Peace Prize, you would:

    A.) Understand that this game could decide whether the Rangers get into the Stanley Cup Playoffs.
    B.) Wish he had an extra ticket so you could go.
    C.) Give his name and address to a high ranking official of the PLO as an "Allah-hater."

6. You compare the Super Bowl to:

    A.) Nirvana and endless orgasms.
    B.) Getting a promotion at work.
    C.) Having four hours of drilling in an abscessed tooth without Novocaine.

7. When deciding on names for your first born and your husband suggests "Willie Mays Johnson" you:

    A.) Agree and suggest Willamina Mays Johnson if it's a girl.
    B.) Try to persuade him that Joe Namath Johnson has a better ring to it.
    C.) Get an abortion.

12

A JOCK ON A DATE

8. When doing word association with your psychiatrist and he or she says the word "sports," you immediately respond:

   A.) Competition
   B.) Athletics
   C.) Severe hemorrhoidal pain

WARNING SIGNS THAT YOU MAY HAVE MET A SPORTS FANATIC

1. When dressed in a tuxedo you notice his socks say "JETS" in green and white.

2. The first time you visit his apartment you notice there's a TV in every room, including the bathroom and closet.

3. You notice he never makes an appointment or date on Sundays from September to January.

4. Your picture is way behind his old high school sports trophies ... they look bright and shiny while your face looks like it needs a shave from all the caked-on dust!

5. When he sees a little boy on the street he refers to him as a "future draft choice."

6. The only time he talks about his mother is when he's telling amusing anecdotes about the great cookies and cakes she used to bake for the team after practices.

7. Whenever he meets a new friend of yours he slaps them so hard on the back that they end up avoiding you like the plague when he's around.

THE PERFECT SUNDAY

	HERS	**HIS**
8:00 A.M.	Jog 3 miles, buy fresh donuts	Sleeping
9:00 A.M.	Read Sunday paper (except sports section)	Still sleeping
10:00 A.M.	Go out with friends for brunch	Stirring
11:00 A.M.	Go shopping at the mall	Stumbles in kitchen for coffee and the sports section
12:00 P.M.	Go visit the new exhibit at the art museum	Read sports section inside out, upside down and backwards, with pre-game show on in the background
1:00 P.M.	Go to local antique shops	Watch first game on TV
2:30 P.M.	Eat lunch at a health-food bistro	(Halftime) Go to the bathroom. Eat hero sandwich with lots of onions while watching and fantasizing over jailbait cheerleaders jiggling up and down
3:00 P.M.	Go to the mall	Watch second half
4:00 P.M.	Workout at gym	Watch next TV sports event
7:00 P.M.	Watch the news, *60 Minutes,* and read new Danielle Steele novel	Watch last game on sports network cable
11:00 P.M.	Go to bed (alone)	Call buddies and discuss highlights of the day's games
11:30 P.M.	Sleep (alone)	Watch sports update & play-by-play on late night news

HOW TO BREAK UP
WITH A SPORTS FANATIC!

Once you have a sports fanatic, you may decide it's time to dump him. Listed below are a few good ways to break it off before you break down!

A. Rent some space on the Goodyear Blimp, so that when he's watching the game he can glance up and see "Sorry, Bob. You blew it! Later, Babbette."

B. Tell him you break out in blotches when watching anything sports related and your psychoanalyst suggests you take a hiatus from sports and sports-related people (Psychosport Syndrome). Given the choice of you or sports, which do you think he would realistically pick?

C. Pack up all your belongings from the apartment and make sure you take the TV, even if it's not yours, because if you don't he'll never even know you're gone!

D. Take out an ad in the sports section saying you've been traded to another team!

E. Send a strip-o-gram explaining things to him during half-time.

18

F. Send him a video cassette of an "instant replay" of you walking out the door giving him the finger!

Remember, if you're feeling lonely after the break—up, all you have to do is place a large male doll in front of your TV and everything will be back to the status quo!!!

CLASSIFIED SINGLES ADS

Life with a sports fanatic will eventually deteriorate to the point where you will be so disgusted with his behavior that placing classified singles ads will begin looking like an attractive option to salvage what's left of your un-social life!

I've pulled a few highly successful versions out of my private files which you can modify according to your personal preferences.

CLASSIFIED EXAMPLE #1

Attractive, sex-starved woman seeks male companion not interested in sports. Can be married, divorced, bankrupt incarcerated, comatose, or even in politics. Minor skin conditions acceptable. I am a Harvard graduate and gourmet cook with lots of money! No prenuptial agreement necessary! Call, write or just drop by! Dial 1–800–IMDESPRIT. Please hurry!

CLASSIFIED EXAMPLE #2

If you're the kind of guy who thinks Mickey Mantle is a place to put Disney pictures on the fireplace, or that Whitey Ford is a car salesman in Harlem, or that Magic Johnson is the name of a porno movie, or that Babe Ruth is a candy bar, or that Larry Bird is a character on *Sesame Street*, or that Sparky Anderson is something you plug into the car's engine, then please call me immediately! Dial 1–800–MELONELY.

THE DIFFERENT TYPES OF SPORTS FANATICS

Your sports fanatic could fall under any of the following fanatic stereotypes, or you may be blessed like I was to find he's a losing combination of them all!

THE JOCK

This is the type of man who just can't leave those glory days of high school and college sports behind him. He still fancies himself a big macho sports participator. You will hardly see him around the house and when you do he'll always be whining about one of his serious injuries received from those tough physical games he plays with his buddies at the park. He will repeatedly give you a blow-by-blow account of each foolish injury until he gets the required proper respect and adoration from you.

If you ever really want a good laugh, dress incognito and follow your sports fanatic to the park and watch the childishly boring game for yourself. Later, back home, you simply won't believe the difference between his version of the grueling action-packed game and your actual observations of what really happens. You'll see a bunch of worn-out, decrepit, no-longer-young men hobbling from goal post to goal post playing "touch" football. These clowns closely resemble your five-year-old's Pee Wee league. But don't ever let on that you know the truth behind their bogus acts—the sports fanatic's fragile ego could never stand it!

A jock's closet

HIS VERSION
OF WHAT HAPPENED

THE TRUTH

"Frank shot me this
awesome bullet pass right
up the center, I jumped
into the air, made the
impossible diving catch and
got tackled hurting my leg,
while scoring in the end zone!"

He ran into a tree!

HIS VERSION OF WHAT HAPPENED	THE TRUTH
"Boy what a great ball game we had. Sorry I'm so late. The score was tied so we had to go into, burp, extra innings!"	The team went out drinking at a sports bar!
"My doctor warned me that I definitely have to give up competitive basketball or I'll have to have knee surgery!"	He never wins one-on-one with the next door neighbor's young son!
"I was walking down the street and this six foot, 350 lb. mugger jumped me from behind, lifted my wallet and ran away."	He lost a big bet on last night's game with his buddies!
"Sorry, honey. I forgot to wear my protective cup during the game— maybe tomorrow!"	He's just too drunk and too tired!
"I've got the kind of body that needs a work out five times a week or I'll lose all my muscle tone!"	The locker rooms at the gym are co-ed!

HIS VERSION OF WHAT HAPPENED

THE TRUTH

"Of course these air pump sneakers are worth $250! They provide awesome support and prevent injuries."

The cute salesgirl with the spandex body suit and plunging cleavage talked me into buying them.

"You know, before I met you I never had to ask permission to play sports with the guys!"

Before he met you his life was a boring, worthless and empty routine revolving around his like-minded, simple, immature high school, college and work buddies.

THE SEASON TICKET HOLDER

This is the really dangerous type who epitomizes fanaticism. He holds the same season tickets year after year, through good times and bad (mostly bad!) just to root for his losing team. The seats are so horrible that by the time you move up one row each year you might reach the fifty yard line by the year 2020.

No use trying to compete with "his" team—you would be better off if he had another woman. At least if he was having an affair you could call up the trollop and have a fight with her. You could also put out a contract on her. But wiping out an entire team would be kind of tough (not to mention expensive). Besides, there'd always be next year's draft!!!

Don't waste time buying this man expensive gifts, like gold rings or cashmere sweaters. He would much prefer mugs, banners, ashtrays and boxer shorts with his team's name plastered all over them.

There is one plus to being with this type of man: you will always be grateful for all the exclusive tailgate parties he uses his influence to attend. And what better place to wear all those new designer clothes you just bought! Make sure that all your clothing is in earth tones and is Scotchguarded because you can never be sure when one of his idiot buddies behind you might spill his mug of beer or up-chuck his peanuts and booze all over you!

THE GAMBLER

Gambling can take many forms, from the guy who plays the weekly office pool all the way to the real he-man who has three or four bookies and bets on just about every game and sport. To test the degree to which your sports fanatic might have this hideous disease, you should take the following True or False Quiz:

DOES THE SPORTS FANATIC YOU KNOW HAVE A GAMBLING PROBLEM?

(BET YOU 2 TO 1 HE DOES!)

1. Does your man regularly make mysterious, quiet, secret phone calls from the other room?

    Yes   No

2. Do you regularly hear the whispered words "vig," "spread" or "over-under" when he's talking to his buddies?

    Yes   No

3. Does the suspected gambling addict occasionally root for teams you've never even heard of, like the Chattanooga Huskies or the Lehigh Engineers?

    Yes   No

4. Does the sports nut occasionally watch a game where he seemingly doesn't care who's winning or losing—just as long as both teams score lots of touchdowns?

    Yes   No

5. Does your sports nerd inexplicably get excited when the team he's cheering for "loses" by 14 points?

    Yes   No

6. Do you ever get strange grunting messages on your answering machine from guys named Louie or Frankie?

    Yes   No

7. When you go out to dinner does the man in question keep disappearing to go to the "restroom" or to wash his hands every fifteen minutes?

    Yes   No

8. When you get your monthly phone bill do you notice one strange number in New Jersey that keeps reappearing, even though you don't know anyone that lives in that state?

    Yes   No

A hard day at the office

9. Do you ever notice that your joint bank account mysteriously goes from your usual state of close to a zero balance to three thousand dollars—and then back to zero in only a two week period?

        Yes   No

10. Have you observed that while your sports addict can't balance his checkbook, he can easily figure the odds on any given horse he and his buddies are discussing?

        Yes   No

RATING YOUR ANSWERS:

If you answered yes to any of the previous questions then you had better get used to spending a lot of time at GAS (Gamblers Anonymous Sidekicks) meetings!

Just a note from experience: make sure you have your own separate savings account in case your sports addict cracks the nest egg and be sure to keep a couple of one-way open tickets to Brazil in your safety deposit box because you never know when Louie or Frankie might come looking for you!

THE SCREAMER-POUNDER

Everyone has met (and wishes they hadn't) someone like this in their lifetime. For me it was Uncle Lefty. (Yes, you guessed it, in Korea he lost his left bun!) When you first met Uncle Lefty he was a very nice, soft-spoken, reasonable gentleman, but turn him loose Sunday afternoon in front of a game on television and you would see a true Dr. Jekyll and Mr. Hyde! When he would start his routine of inane barking like a jackal, any sane person would have to run out of the room and hide! My Aunt finally had to seek help from the church because even the psychiatrists couldn't do anything to help her sports fool's worsening emotional problem, which manifested itself only while he watched his games on TV. Out of desperation she begged the church to intercede and assist her family with their problem. The church reluctantly gave her the go-ahead to perform one of its rare sports exorcisms. I heard it was a very gruesome affair: all sorts of unpleasant odors filled the room. The smell was supposedly similar to the men's room urinals at Yankee Stadium on a hot August

*Sometimes you can detect a difference in a man's behavior
once the game starts.*

day. Fortunately, the exorcism worked for Uncle Lefty, however, the poor priest who performed the ritualistic ceremony somehow got infected with the disease and he's now running his own private Off Track Betting establishment in Los Angeles!

Below is a profile of the typical Screamer-Pounder. If you get to know the warning signs it might make it easier for you to avoid this fanatic, just as you would any other dangerous psychopathic maniac!

THE SCREAMER-POUNDER PROFILE

Age—4 to 98 years old (they peak at thirtysomething!).

Weight—Forty pounds over the national average for their age.

Known Associates—Four or five men with similar builds who are always toting a six-pack or two (or three or four!).

Favorite Phrases—Sh__ , F__ , Jerk O__ or A__ H__ . Can also be heard belching or farting during commercials.

Favorite Foods—Pretzels, potato chips, beer nuts, nacho chips, guacomole dip, beef jerky or any food high in poly-saturated fat that clots the arteries and produces excessive natural gas explosions in human beings.

Physical Traits—Popping Fresh Doughboy-appearance, bloodshot eyes from too many hours of sports viewing, giant pulsating veins on forehead, remote control permanently attached to right hand, and if you look very carefully under his hair line—if he's still lucky enough to have one!—you'll find three small birthmarks in the shape of tiny footballs!

Below is a list of dos and don'ts that every woman should know if she's involved with the "Screamer-Pounder." Your safety may be at stake with this type of sports fanatic!

DO be sure that the TV viewing area is far away from the rest of the house and if possible have it sound-proofed. You will always be able to use it later when your son decides he wants to take up lead guitar for Twisted Sister! (And remember to keep your cool, because this is a lot better than your son playing high school football!)

DON'T feel slighted when some of the words he yells out during the game are the very same ones you remember hearing when he reaches one of his rare orgasms.

DO remove hands and yourself quickly when bringing over any food for consumption by "the boys." You'll be lucky to come away unscarred or unspattered by these prehistoric buffoons.

Rodger Remote

Mom's reliable baby sitter.

DON'T leave any small children for your sports fanatic to baby-sit or you're likely to come home and find them (if they're still breathing) completely unsupervised doing cute little things like torturing the family pets and each other.

DON'T ever embarrass your sports imbecile during a game by asking him to explain, in front of his important company, why the funny man in the silly black and white suit is waving the little yellow flag! Better yet, don't ask any questions at all about the game—just be a good little waitress and keep the food and drinks coming and clean up the mess at half-times or as time-outs allow.

37

DON'T let him catch you going through the *TV Guide*. If it's not within his reach he could reach for your throat instead!

DO stock up on all his favorite munchies and beer because if he runs out during an important game he'll break into one of your fifty-year-old bottles of Dom Perignon, one you've been saving for a special occasion. He'll chug it down with the boys in a few seconds, just like they do with good beer. (If this does happen don't be too concerned— you'll never have a special occasion to celebrate with this guy anyway!)

DON'T embarrass yourself by letting the girls at the nail salon know that your sports fanatic monopolizes the TV and watches hours and hours of idiotic sporting events. Instead tell them that he watches PBS—but don't let on that it stands for Professional Bullshit Sports!

DON'T have sexual relations with the Screamer-Pounder after he watches a game where his team has just lost— unless you're into really rough sex (which is better than no sex at all!).

THE POOR LOSER

Some types of gamblers you can live with but never ever even think of marrying the "poor loser!" He is basically the most pathetic, miserable creature of all mankind (and I've described a lot so far in this book). If you are lucky you can spot the "poor loser" ahead of time.

Here follows the warning signs.

1. He has absolutely no male friends who hang out with him while rooting for sporting events. (Not even his dog will stay around when he's watching a game!)

2. He has an idiotic, illogical, weak excuse for every losing game. Example: "I should have know better than to bet on the Cleveland Browns, brown has always been my worst color!" Or "My horoscope said 'Beware of Leo, he is not to be trusted' and of course Leo is a lion which means I should never have bet on those lousy Detroit Lions!"

3. He still plays the videotape of the losing high school game where he was wide open and dropped the winning pass in the end zone. He watches it over and over again from every angle trying to figure out *who* really screwed up.

4. He always doubles his bets to try to make up for his losing game—which makes him doubly pissed off later when he loses again!

5. He watches *Rocky* before each game and listens to the James Bond theme music—just to get himself properly "pumped up."

6. He insists all the games are "fixed" by the same people responsible for the JFK and RFK conspiracies and cover-ups.

7. He blames all his bad luck and losing bets on you !

THE VCR FANATIC

You're one of the lucky ones. This sports fanatic will go places with you on occasion and hang-out with you while you do "your" womanly things, as long as he can tape the game. The only problem is when you're out with this schmuck you can't be anywhere near a TV or radio. Every conversation he starts with a friend, relative or stranger will begin with

"Don't tell me the score of the game—and don't even give me a hint!"

Inevitably, at the end of the evening after constant idiotic hints and subtle pressure, someone will say, "I won't tell you the score but the tenth inning was a real nail-biter!" You know, being the intelligent woman that you are (of course how intelligent can you be if you're hooked up with a loser sports fanatic!), that this JERK blew the whole game for your man and you may never be able to tape a game and go out again! (For your information, baseball games are only nine innings so if the game went into the tenth, that means the score was tied. So now your reluctant date has little enjoyment watching the first nine innings he taped!)

THE MALE BONDER

The hardest type of man for a sports widow to handle is the male bonder. I don't know about you but somehow I feel really cheated when I see the ease with which this otherwise tight-lipped man can relate to perfect strangers!

For example you hop into a taxi and glance at the driver's name on the dashboard and you see his last name is Dpxxzrzzkk and he's wearing a large towel wrapped around his head (a clue that he's not originally from this country). A normal person would simply sit back and watch the passing scenery, hoping not to be involved in any crashes or terrorist incidents. A male-bonding sports fanatic, on the other hand, would immediately launch into, "So what do you think of those Giants" and the next thing you know these two culturally different misfits would suddenly carry on a twenty-minute conversation that even the interpreters at the

*Hey Father, forget the Last Rites,
how about those Rangers?*

United Nations wouldn't be able to decode!

I'm sorry but I can't picture getting into a cab with a female driver and saying "So what do you think of the price of those new Chanel bags advertised in *Vogue*? I mean we just don't have that universal idiotic tie to keep us in the same fraternity that sophisticated sports minded men do!

THE OCCASIONAL SPORTSMAN (EVERY WOMAN'S DREAM!!)

Somewhere out there, some place, there must exist the occasional sportsman. I've heard some friends call their boyfriends this, but I don't think they're telling the truth or they wouldn't be calling me to go out with them every other night.

There are rumors that in a remote part of the New Hampshire mountains there is a colony of these special men who really, truly are "occasional sportsmen." They keep to themselves, and from what I've heard they are the perfect male specimens. Unfortunately, as is usually the case with the good ones, they are of course all happily married—just like Mel Gibson, Kevin Costner and Paul Newman.

WHAT HE DOES

Sends flowers for every special event

Goes on family outings— even on major "sports weekends"

Donates his spare time to help clean up the environment

WHAT HE DOESN'T DO

Belches while watching "the game"

Passes gas loudly in public while watching "the game"

Hits the arm of the easy chair and table when his team misses a play

WHAT HE DOES

Supports animal rights
and is against using
products that experiment
on animals

Actually cries at the end
of sad movies

Likes to wallpaper and
enjoys painting the house

Regularly takes the kids to
the zoo and museum

Frequently cooks
gourmet meals

Occasionally watches the
final deciding game of the
World Series and the
Super Bowl and prefers
to spend quality time
with his family

WHAT HE DOESN'T DO

Curses loudly whenever the
side he is rooting for makes
an error

Pounds the dog when his
team gets a penalty

Throws sneakers at the TV
when his team messes up
big-time

Throws junior at the TV
when the umpire makes
a bad call

Pulls at his hair
when his team loses
the advantage

Pulls your hair out
when his team loses
the game

SURE-TO-GET-A-LAUGH SPORTS JOKES

It's important to be able to laugh at your dismal situation when dealing with the effect sports widowhood has had on your life. I've collected a few sports jokes that I use to help me make light of a usually very dark situation. You should share them with a fellow widow or even use them in conversation with your pathetic sports fanatic.

SILLY SPORTS JOKES

From what ailment did the pitcher and his pregnant wife both suffer?
Complete exhaustion in the ninth.

What's the difference between baseball and dating?
On a date, the man still does all the pitching ... but it's the woman who has the best curves.

When room service arrived with the Major League baseball star's breakfast, the waiter saw a dress, blouse and female undergarments scattered around the room.

"Would you like me to bring anything for your wife?" the waiter innocently inquired.

The player's brow furrowed, and he handed the waiter a five dollar bill. "Good idea. Bring me some postcards from the newsstand."

A sports fanatic confessed to his wife, "I dream about baseball every night."

His wife asked, "don't you dream about anything else?"

"What? And miss my turn at bat!"

What's the first thing aspiring cheerleaders and aspiring players must do before they can become stars?
They both have to make the team.

Why did the weightlifter enjoy going to singles' joints?
He liked picking up bar belles.

A University coach was being interviewed by a sports-caster and he got sick and tired of hearing about how dumb football players were so he cited a survey he'd recently read.

"According to a CBS poll, over half of the young men who play college ball are making A's and B's."

"That's wonderful," said the cynical interviewer. "The question is, when will they learn to write the rest of the alphabet?"

What's the toughest challenge most pro linemen ever have to face?
Graduating the sixth grade.

When does a musclebound lowlife become a body builder?
When he marries your daughter.

Why do football players wear helmets?
So they don't wipe the wrong end.

A less-than-brilliant football player sat heavily on the bar stool, in a depressed mood and with a gloomy expression on his face.

"Hey, why so down?" the bartender asked. "I read that you just got engaged."

"Nah ... it's off," said the player.

"That's too bad. What happened?"

"She admitted she loved another man."

"No kidding?"

"Nope. Last night, she told me she'd be true to the end."

The bartender scratched his head. "So what's wrong with that?"

"I'm the quarterback."

After a tiring day of watching football on TV, a sports fanatic fell asleep in his easy chair. Instead of waking him, his wife let him sleep and she went to bed.

The next morning, she found him still snoozing away in his chair.

Nudging him gently, she softly said, "Wake up, dear. It's twenty to seven."

The sports fanatic was startled, and yelled out, "Whose favor?"

What's the quarterback's least favorite dessert?
Turnovers.

One sport widow said to another, "After twenty years of marriage, our sex life is just like the Super Bowl."

"You mean the noise, the excitement, the fun."

"No," she said. "I mean it happens just once a year."

What's the difference between a man who makes love like an artist and one who makes love like a golfer?

The artist strokes for hours, while the golfer wants to get into the hole in as few strokes as possible.

The playboy hockey star was sent to the hospital with a concussion.

After looking in on him, one nurse was stopped by another. "Is he making any progress?" she asked.

"He's trying," said the other, "but I prefer going out with a man who has all his teeth."

What do you need when you come across a sports fanatic buried to his chin in cement?

More cement.

What's the difference between a sports fanatic and a pothole?

You'd swerve to avoid a pothole.

What do you call three sports fanatics sinking in quicksand?

A good start.

Who is John McEnroe's greatest fan?

His wife's husband.

SPORTSBUSTER: THE ANTI-SPORTS MAGAZINE

SPORTS BUSTER

Sally Rafanatic
Interviews
Seymour Sports

Sports Abuse:
One Woman's Hell

Plus:
Dear Crabby
Horoscope
and More

SPORTS FANATIC SWIMSUIT EDITION
ALSO: OUR SIZZLING SPORTLESS MALE CENTERFOLD

am convinced that a good way to cope with a sports-aholic would be the availability of a slick anti-sports magazine for suffering sports widows. Here's a sample of what you'd find in each issue of *Sportsbuster Magazine*.

57

Letter From The Editor

As Editor of *Sportsbuster,* I think it's important to point out that we can not put all the blame for sports fanaticism on our men. Some mention must be made of those certain females who ruin it for us all! I'm talking about messed-up mothers, wimpy wives, cheeky cheerleaders, sexless sportscasters and female fanatics. These women are our enemies, they have been making it impossible to get anywhere in this sports crazed world. As long we have breath in our lungs I think it's imperative that we stand together as sisters and fight these women every step of the way!

I don't know about you, but as long as there are mothers and wives who wait hand and foot on these poor pathetic men watching game after game—we will never be free! And those bouncy, jiggling, pubescent cheerleaders will never blaze the path for sportless Saturdays and Sundays. And think of a female and male—jockette and jock—couple, can you imagine inviting them over on the weekend? Your man will take one look at her and he'll be placing ads in the classifieds for a carbon copy! Furthermore, the induction of more and more female sportscasters is making it very hard for the men in this world to believe that we just don't have it in our genes to enjoy sports!

I would enjoy hearing from any of our readers who

have any ideas on how we can take care of this insidious problem. Let's not just do it for us but let's do it for our children!

Sally Jesse Rafanatic Interviews Seymour Sports

Sally Jesse Rafanatic: Okay, Seymour Sports, our readership really wants to know what makes a man like you tick? First of all why don't you tell us a little about your childhood—where did you grow up, what were your parents like, and who was responsible for turning you on to sports?

Seymour Sports: Well Mrs. Rafanatic—I'm sorry, I know you liberated types like to be called Ms.— which I think must have been originally derived from the last two letters of PMS! Anyway, I grew up in Hogseed, Iowa—I'm sure you've heard of it—you know it's just outside of Buckeye Country! My father was the best dad around and I remember being about a year old—things were pretty tough back then we hillbillies barely had enough food to feed ourselves ... that is me and my ten brothers. Good ole Mom had just enough kids to qualify as a football team!

Well, one day Dad and my Uncle Shlep decided that just because we couldn't afford a football, it shouldn't stop us from having fun. So my Dad took me outside, told me to huddle real small, and started heaving me across the yard to my Uncle. I remember the rush of flying through the air, back and forth from one man to the other, faster than a speeding bullet! People would come from all over the county just to see the "Human Football." My brothers would collect the money from our little act and Mom would serve weenies and beer with great big foaming heads. Boy, those were the good old days!

SJR: You mean your mother actually let your father abuse you and throw you like that—I mean what kind of sadistic mother would encourage such a thing!

SS: Hey, don't you put down my Ma, she knew her place. What my Pop said, well that was the law, just like it's supposed to be. All Dad had to do was say to Mom, "Boy it sure would be nice to have a special field kicker on our team." Mom would shut her mouth and her eyes would start to glaze over. There were no liberationists in our family, let me tell you, we were a good ole American, God-fearing family—with traditional sports-lovin' values.

SJR: Okay, enough about your unbearable childhood. Tell us about other women in your life, how do you make them happy and what place do they share in your life?

SS: I thought this article was supposed to be about sports, not women!!!

SJR: Yes, but our readers would appreciate some insight on how to understand your psyche.

SS: Psyche, what is that one of those new sneakers?

SJR: No, we want to know why sports is so important in your life so that our readers might better understand people like you.

SS: Sports isn't just important in my life, it IS my life!

SJR: What kind of women really turn you on?

SS: All kind of women make me hot, um I mean turn me on.

SJR: Yea, I'm sure you like them as long as the TV's not "turned on!" What's your idea of the perfect evening with a special woman?

SS: Well, I can tell from your tone that you probably think I would say I would take her to some sporting event for hot dogs and beer. Well, I prefer to keep my women friends away from sports—it's something I think only men can share and properly understand. I would take her to a nice quiet dinner and dancing of course!

SJR: Really. How often does a guy like you do that?

SS: Well, New Year's Eve of course. And on her birthday, if it happens to fall on a day when there's no game on the tube.

SJR: Did you ever think she might want to share some of your interests and that perhaps she is actually interested in partaking in a hot weenie and something with lots of head on it?

SS: Hey you brazen hussy. Don't talk dirty to me, I know when someone's trying to jerk my chain—I'm much deeper than you feminists realize!

SJR: Right! You're about as deep and as understanding of women and as desirable to date as Mike Tyson.

SS: Well, thanks Sally, it's about time you paid me a compliment and stopped trying to make me look bad.

SJR: On that note, I think it's time to end this stimulating interview. Thank you for giving our readers such wonderful insight into the complex thinking of the "sports fanatic."

Dear Crabby

Dear Crabby

My wedding date is quickly approaching and I know it's only normal to get last minute jitters, but last night I had the most horrible dream. I dreamt it was my wedding night and things were going pretty well when all of a sudden my man's handsome face turned into this gruesome mask of ugliness. I started screaming and running for the door but he kept following me, talking with this garbled raspy voice. In my horror, right before I woke up I realized who he had turned into—yes, you guessed it—PETE ROSE!!! Do you think this dream could be a message that I should not marry someone like my fiancé whose entire life revolves around sports? He promises me he will reform his sports fanatic ways after we are married.

Signed,
Scared of Sports

Dear Scared,

Yes, I think you should be a little concerned about this dream and also about your supposed "Dreamboat." As we all know, few, if any men change after they get married. If anything, they get worse because now they no longer need to impress you by showing any caring or depth of character after getting what they want from you—food, maid service, and a little sex. My suggestion would be a pre-nuptial agreement that would simply limit the amount of sports in your future man's miserable life! You should be sure to include a clause in the contract that states: "The aforementioned male shall only be permitted to view sporting events once a week on TV or videotape. Twice a month he will be permitted to go to live sporting events, only on week days and without *the company of his mate. When watching sports in his own home, he is limited to inviting two male companions unless special permission is given by his mate with one week advanced written notice. By signing this document, it is agreed that all claims to his estate and assets will be given up and his wife will be released from any and all financial obligations incurred by him in his various sports betting investments and speculations."*

A pre-nuptial agreement like this is worth more than any phony liquid assets your lover may otherwise promise you. What you should be concerned about are football passes. I would also strongly suggest you contact your clergyman and request a modification in your marriage vows so they go something like this: "For richer or poorer, in sickness and in health, in football and in hockey, but NO BASEBALL."

Dear Crabby,

I am writing this letter because I'm at the end of my rope and it's going to be the same rope I put around my husband's neck. He is a very sick sports-aholic!!! If he's not watching it, he's reading it and the only time he notices me is when he compares my cellulite to the firm skin on the cheerleaders' thighs or he reaches out to give me a squeeze while staring at and fantasizing over the jiggling, bursting, supple chests of the bouncing cheerleaders. Help!

Signed,

Hopelessly Depressed

Dear Depressed,

Things are looking pretty bleak so I would suggest a trial separation (from TV). If your husband cannot do this cold turkey, I would cut down his sports supply on a daily basis, eliminating one game at a time. It's also a good idea to reduce the size of his viewing area—cut down to a 12-inch screen then, perhaps a "Watchman." If this doesn't work I would suggest you get aid from some self-help groups such as Athletics Anonymous or W.A.S.T.E. (Women Against Sports Television Enjoyment)! Lastly, remind your man about the worsening AIDS and sexually transmitted disease epidemics and emphasize how these slutty cheerleaders obviously are "doing" the entire team while also servicing the team's owners and friends of the owners. Then ask him if he really would consider it wise, in this age of social diseases, to lust after these walking sleazettes of doom!

Dear Crabby,

I am writing this letter in hope that I may help other women with a tried and true recipe for curbing men from becoming sports addicts. Recently my boyfriend and I agreed on a compromise that has completely changed our lives.

Here's how it works: Every time your man wants to watch a sporting event on TV, you simply tell him as a compromise he must watch a Barbra Streisand movie in return, and if he watches sports all day, you expect in return that he watch, with you, a Meryl Streep film festival including such tear jerkers as *Sophie's Choice, Silkwood, Kramer vs. Kramer,* and *The French Lieutenant's Woman!*

I guarantee you that he'll think twice before he puts on some un-important small fry college game! I hope your readers will take heart and try to learn my new motto: "Threaten him with Streep and he won't make a peep!"

Signed,
Happy at Last

Dear Happy,

Thank you for your wise advice, I'm sure you have helped a lot of women. Please don't forget to add Ironweed *and* Heartburn *to your hit parade. Make 'em suffer!*

Your Man's Horoscope

Capricorn—Dec. 22 to Jan. 20 (The Goat): This guy is a real climber! He makes his way up the social ladder by constantly talking sports nonsense with his superiors, trying to impress them with his knowledge of trivia and minutiae about current important topics in sports. He is one of those who constantly reads idiotic sports statistics out loud in the office and listens to boring pre-game shows just to get the edge over the other sports buffs at work. A real worthless bore!

Aquarius—Jan. 21 to Feb. 19 (The Water Bearer): This guy lives his life on the sidelines. When he was young his one claim to fame was being the water boy for his little league team (he was never good enough to play). At college he was a male cheerleader—you know the type. In other words he's always been a wimp and a dreamer—he's never accomplished anything in sports that he wanted to. So be smart by staying away from this frustrated, unsatisfied, sure-to-be impotent, inexperienced, weak excuse of a man!

Pisces—Feb. 20 to March 20 (The Fish): Just like a fish doesn't do well out of water, this guy doesn't perform well when not discussing sports. He can carry on any conversation intelligently if it's related to sports, but try to change the subject and you'll see him floundering on shore gasping for breath! His relationship to sports is a substitute for his lack of other interests in life and is what enables this loser to continue his insignificant existence. Instead of sex this type satisfies himself with "orgies" of TV sports climaxing with special sports cable channels and pay-per-view events. Given the choice to play with his date, to play with himself or to play with his TV's remote control unit—he'll go for the TV every time. Avoid this royal pain in the behind! Lose this loser.

Aries—March 21 to April 20 (The Ram): This man is similar to the frat boys in *Animal House*. Like a ram he gets great pleasure butting beer cans with his head in front of his buddies during an important game. Try not to tangle horns with these mental midgets! Not only are their minds tiny, but so is their sexual desire and their capacity to please women. All of those wasted hours in front of the TV set and its dangerous radiation emissions has permanently damaged this guy's ability to perform—except when it comes to acting like an imbecile while watching sports with his moronic friends.

Taurus—April 21 to May 21 (The Bull): This guy's the big bragger. He goes around constantly telling all those boring stories of his glory days playing college sports. In other words he's full of "bull," full of himself and incapable of knowing what a woman wants—let alone being able to perform, should the rare opportunity present itself. Watch out for these types that talk the most—as they usually deliver the least!

Gemini—May 22 to June 21 (The Twins): If you hook up with a Gemini you'd better be prepared to

hook up with his bosom buddy also. His friend will be the type of "twin" who sleeps on your couch and eats all your food. You'll rarely get a word in because the two of them will be continuously working on their relationship and discussing sports. I would suggest encouraging them to sleep in the same bed together so they get so much of each other's company that if they really want their sick sports-based friendship to become sexual, you will find out sooner rather than later. If these two are sexually compatible, you can end your useless relationship while there's still plenty of time for you to find a normal, non-sports oriented man—something you should have done in the first place. Beware of this trash!!!

Cancer—June 22 to July 23 (The Crab): Just like the disease and the itchy discomfort, it's hard to get rid of this dude. He'll embed himself into the fibers of your sofa while watching his idiotic sporting events on TV, and you'll have a hard time prying him loose for the rest of your relationship! If you let this couch potato into your home, expect him to sprout sports spores that wrap like tentacles around your television set. On his rare sojourns away from the sofa, you'll find the only thing this Crab uses his pincers for is to tweak the cheeks of the barmaid at the local sports bar!

Leo—July 23 to Aug. 23 (The Lion): This man's sign should be changed to "the pig." He thinks he's "the king of the jungle" and will use his giant paws to swipe you out of the way of the TV. His chauvinistic attitude is what women have been fighting against for years—put a muzzle on that big trap of his and hope that Tarzan swings down from a vine and saves you from this lion's den!

Virgo—Aug. 24 to Sept. 23 (The Virgin): This guy is a winner—the real thing!!! His mind is "sports free." Just make sure you keep him away from any kind of pro-sports environment—unplug the TV and radio in your apartment and hide all the sports sections in the daily newspaper. As a test, ask this man who Merle Olsen is. If he answers "the guy on *Little House* *on the Prairie*" then you know you're okay! Finding a "sports virgin" has many more rewards than you might imagine—his easy-to-mold personality makes him "putty" in your hands. I'm sure you will find a few warm places this putty can be formed to fit!!

Libra—Sept. 24 to Oct. 23 (The Scales of Justice): As you've probably already noticed, men who fall under this sign are smitten with an interesting streak of fairness in their character. For every game you are forced to watch, they'll let you watch an equivalent number of hours of your favorite programs. This can be a pleasant change for you—but watch out for their sneaky charms. While they are watching your favorite Meryl Streep movies and preferred sitcoms, the Libra male will be busy calculating how much sex you owe him in return for his suffering. And they'll be so smooth in putting their guilt trip on you that you won't be able to turn them down. At least these sports fanatics' minds are in the right places.

Scorpio—Oct. 24 to Nov. 22 (The Scorpion): In the case of the Scorpio, his stinger is not what you think it might be! This man's mind, like other sports fanatics, is not in the bedroom, but in the family room! He likes to poison all impressionable young minds around him with his single-minded view of sports! I would suggest if you hook up with this loser of a Neanderthal you had better find yourself an antidote quickly.

Sagittarius—Nov. 23 to Dec. 21 (The Archer): The male Sagittarian is the most athletic sign of them all. Always keep in mind that a Sagittarian is half horse and half archer and you can rest assured that this sports fanatic is definitely the horse's ass! The one time you can be sure you won't see him performing any outstanding physical moves is when it's time for love-making! This guy is no stallion—he's more like an old rundown little burro when it comes to pleasing women. Don't let this impotent steroid-stud shoot an arrow anywhere near your heart or you will quickly live to regret the experience!

Sportsbuster's Special Edition: Sports Fanatics Swimsuit Issue

The Sportsless Male Centerfold: Mr. October, Sensitive Sylvester

Hobbies: Ballet, Opera, Antiquing, Art History

Favorite Books: *Love Story, The Story of Susan B. Anthony, Gone With the Wind, How TV Ruins the Mind, Sexually Pleasing Your Woman 24-Hours-a-Day* and anything by Judith Krantz

Favorite Foods: Quiche, Souffles, Garden Salads and Yogurt

Favorite Movies: *Terms of Endearment, Places in the Heart, Endless Love*

Sports Abuse: The Story of One Woman's Harrowing Hell

Mrs. Mabel Smith, a seemingly shy and demure housewife from Hoboken, New Jersey, was accused of murdering her husband, Fred, by repeatedly bashing him with his own sharp baseball cleats while he was dozing in his "Lazy Boy" watching the third game of the World Series. What would cause a perfectly respectable woman to perform these drastic violent acts? On the next pages is a flow chart that will show how something like this can happen and perhaps help you from making the same mistake and falling into a similar trap.

Sports Abuse Flow Chart

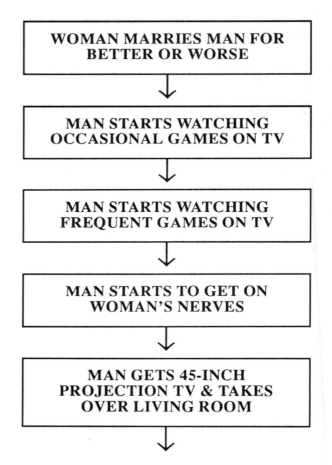

WOMAN MARRIES MAN FOR
BETTER OR WORSE

↓

MAN STARTS WATCHING
OCCASIONAL GAMES ON TV

↓

MAN STARTS WATCHING
FREQUENT GAMES ON TV

↓

MAN STARTS TO GET ON
WOMAN'S NERVES

↓

MAN GETS 45-INCH
PROJECTION TV & TAKES
OVER LIVING ROOM

↓

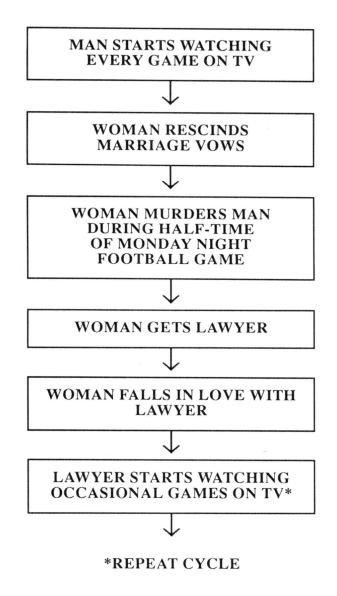

MAN STARTS WATCHING
EVERY GAME ON TV

WOMAN RESCINDS
MARRIAGE VOWS

WOMAN MURDERS MAN
DURING HALF-TIME
OF MONDAY NIGHT
FOOTBALL GAME

WOMAN GETS LAWYER

WOMAN FALLS IN LOVE WITH
LAWYER

LAWYER STARTS WATCHING
OCCASIONAL GAMES ON TV*

*REPEAT CYCLE

COPING WITH A SPORTS FANATIC

MOPE AROUND THE DOPE

It's Sunday morning and deep depression sets in. You know he plans on endlessly watching game after game on the tube. The sun is shining and the birds are chirping, so what do you, as an intelligent woman, do? You can walk around bored and despondent, wearing one of his old jerseys, your hair hanging limply in front of your face, covering your permanent scowl in anticipation of the wasted day that is about to happen. You've made the decision—the wrong decision—that it's better to be with your boring, uncaring sports fanatic, even though he's such a schmuck that he doesn't even acknowledge your existence.

This is what clinical psychologists call the "Mope Around the Dope Syndrome"! I have listed several proven alternatives to moping around the dope. Hopefully, one of them will work for you!

1. AMERICAN EXPRESSION FOR YOUR DEPRESSION

Shopping is an age-old solution to the problems confronting today's sports widows. The advantage to this technique is instant gratification. The disadvantage, of course, is your monthly charge statements. You probably won't have the occasion to wear what you buy because your mate's rear end is permanently attached to the easy chair in front of the

"Now I know why they call it Victoria's Secret"

TV. But let me tell you, what a charge he'll get when he goes over the monthly bills. He may think twice next time he decides to ruin your weekend when he ends up with the choice between the "Forty Niners" and "forfeiture."

Clothing is not the only thing you can shop around for.* If you have the extra cash why not go out and get yourself a sports-free gigolo who can satisfy those sexual desires that your man no longer is capable of handling! Make it a condition of payment that the Gigolo must not mention anything sports related. Don't worry about your sports fanatic catching the two of you in the sack—if he finds out he'll probably be euphoric that he can now devote more time to his sports.

Just a little tip that might help you to save a bit of extra cash for your family. Refill the empties of his favorite beer with the cheapest brand you can find. You pocket the savings and he'll never notice the difference!

2. MINGLE WITH A SINGLE

Everyone has a girlfriend who's playing the field. She can fill your head with amusing anecdotes of life in the fast lane and go into Technicolor detail about the hunt for the perfect male. While your sports fanatic is at home glued to the game, you can go out with your friend to a singles bar, slip off your wedding ring and pretend for one glorious night that you didn't make the mistake of your life marrying a self-absorbed, boring, sports slob. Unfortunately, the bar most likely contains a television which just happens to have a football game on, that just happens to hold the attention of all the eligible men you are trying to attract!

If you pay too much attention to all of those horrible stories about fooling around in this age of sexually transmitted diseases, you may realize that life as a sports widow isn't as bad as you thought. You'll never have to worry about getting AIDS from your sports fanatic. You'll be lucky if he gets close enough to give you the common cold!

3. BECOME A TENNIS MENACE

There are two ways you can go about doing this. One is to ask around, find the best instructor in your area and learn how to play the game to fill all those boring hours while your sports fanatic ignores you. Each time you slam the ball try to imagine that you are hitting your sports fanatic's chubby little face!

The other alternative is to find an instructor who just happens to be gorgeous and flirtatious—don't worry if he's

a good tennis player on the court as long as he knows how to play off the court! This will help you cope when you have to go home to Mr. Boring—whenever he mentions sports you just let your mind wander to your new sport—your tennis pro! Looks like now the score will be tied at Love-All!

4. COOK BY THE BOOK

Becoming a gourmet is a good way to spend your free time. Perhaps some of your aromatic delicacies will tempt him enough to lift his butt off his TV easy chair. Unfortunately, I have never enjoyed a gourmet meal yet that was under five thousand calories and, I'm sorry, but the "Weight Watchers Cookbook" just doesn't make it! Do not attempt to cook if your kitchen is next to the den. It's hard to enjoy preparing

85

gastronomical delights when from the next room you hear loud shouting, screaming and don't forget the ever popular BELCH!

I devised the following little recipe for those times when you've just about had it whipping up food for your fat fanatic's feasting rituals. Serve this just once and he and his buddies will never bother you again—and the good thing is they can't say you were purposely out to get them, because all the ingredients are the ones they love!! One hint, however, make sure you leave the house. Better yet, leave the county, because when this diabolical delicacy hits their lower intestines you won't want to be around for the fall-out! And they thought Chernobyl was a catastrophe.

RECIPE FOR TUBE STEAK DIJON

INGREDIENTS:

6 pkgs. of "Ball Fart" Weenies
2 pkgs. of "Poopsie's" Special Sauerkraut
18 Onions
2 Jars of "Poop-on" Mustard
1 can of stale "Bores" Beer
3 cans of "Bubba's Best" Bean Mix

DIRECTIONS:

Put all of the ingredients in your food processor and blend until you have a smooth greenish-brown paste. Let the mixture sit at room temperature on the counter until it becomes crusty at the edges. Allow the family dog or cat to have a little nibble of the finished product. If they belch appropriately then you can chill and serve. If they don't, add more onions and sauerkraut and then serve it to the animals again. If they roll over and play dead, use less sauerkraut. It is now ready to be served to your sports fanatic and his sports-loving guests.

5. LEARN A LINGO

Learning a foreign language is a good way to expand your horizons while your couch potato sits and rots! Perhaps you could use this time to plan a nice trip to some exotic country, but make sure the place you pick has not even heard of electricity. Also, make sure you schedule your trip between sports seasons.* An advantage to learning a new language is the fact that you can practice at home using earphones, thus

* *See Sports Spread Sheet*

Below is a sports spread sheet that can help you plan
your calendar. This will let you know, depeding on
what sport your fanatic is into, what time you can plan
to spend alone with him without the threat of sports
viewing! If you are still in the dating mode, this can
help you decide whether to dump the jerk or not!

SPORTS SPREAD SHEET

	Football	BASEball	BASketball	Golf	Hockey	P/Os*
JAN	X		X		X	X
FEB			X		X	X
MAR			X		X	X
APR		X	X		X	X
APRIL²**						
MAY		X	X	X		X
JUNE		X	X	X		X
JULY		X		X		X
AUG	X	X		X		X
SEPT	X	X				X
OCT	X	X	X			X
NOV	X		X		X	X
DEC	X		X		X	X

* Play-offs—Don't even think of Human interaction on these dates!
** April 2nd—Maybe a good day to plan your vacation!

drowning out all those obnoxious background sports noises from your mate.

If you pick French as your foreign lingo, you can combine this with shopping. You'll finally be able to pronounce all those designer names without a single "faux pas!"

6. LINK WITH A SHRINK

Seeing a psychiatrist is nothing to be ashamed of compared to living in the shadow of your sports fanatic's tyranny. It's always good to have a shrink in your life because you never know when your mind will snap and you'll be facing the death penalty for murdering your mate. You might need your doctor to vouch for the fact that your mate's sports-abusing personality was the reason for your breakdown and the justification for your uncontrollable violence. If you're lucky enough to get a woman judge at your trial maybe you'll have a chance

to cop a plea like "not-guilty by reason of extreme and unusual over-exposure to sports."

7. START WITH ART

Even if you are not artistically inclined, drawing can be a very therapeutic means of expression. Make sure the first class you take is "How to Draw the Human Form 101" and also be sure that they have nude male models that resemble Adonis. You should be cautious as this may be the first time you've seen a naked man that doesn't have a giant beer belly. (Make sure you have a hankie to wipe any drool that may form in the corner of your mouth!) It may also bring back memories of your man's body when you first met, when he was in good shape for the "babes"—before he started his ritual of "Football Feasting." This can be a very nice way to spend an afternoon, not to mention how easy it is on your eyes and libido!!!

8. MAYBE A BABY

When all else fails to fill the lonely time in your life, getting pregnant and having children is always a great way to keep yourself busy on Monday nights and weekends. If you plan this correctly you'll be so nauseous and busy, you won't even notice the sports seasons as they come and go! Just remember though, if you're not careful you might be creating little clones of your sports fanatic mate—which could make life in the future even more unbearable! Make sure you have at least one girl so you can have someone besides your mother to complain to!

9. BEGIN A BUSINESS

If you are not already employed in a wonderful non-sports related career, you may want to take some time out and think about opening your own business—the choices are endless. I started my own business a few years ago. The parent company, called Sabotage, Inc., is based solely on the premise that sports widows will pay anything to get back at their sports fanatic husbands—especially after the divorce. (You bought this book didn't you!) My company produces Anti-Sports videos, books and visual aids. I also started a computer service that lets sports widows pipe into a special program where they can compare all their mates' sports atrocities with other widows. Not only can you relate to the other abused widows but you can also share recipes on how to get even or how to get their attention. Below is a list I've compiled from the Sports Widow Network of tried and true evil practical jokes you can pull on your very own sports fanatic!

EVIL PRACTICAL JOKES

A. Hide the sports section of the Sunday paper. Pretend you never saw it and blame it on the poor defenseless newspaper delivery kid. A good place is in the bushes under the drain pipe, so if he does find it, the paper's too wet and damp to read anyway.

B. Tape a soap opera right in the middle of a game he taped the night before. You can only use this act a couple of

times, but believe me there's nothing funnier than seeing him watch the tape, getting more and more involved in the game, when all of a sudden the screen changes to Erica and Devon rolling around in bed moaning and groaning in ecstasy!

C. While he's getting ready to settle down for a long day of sports viewing, slip a laxative into his beer. It will be fun to see him running back and forth from the bathroom to the television missing lots of key plays!

D. Send a fake indictment citing your man's involvement in a gambling investigation. Be sure to link him with some of the names of guys he places his usual bets with, like Louie and Frankie!

E. Have the cable repair man show you how to disconnect the cable from the outside of the house. Do it on a Friday so you can have a sports-free weekend—then go to the video store and rent some really good romantic comedies or porno movies!

F. Sit your sports fanatic down for a serious talk about your son. Scare him by telling him that your son has decided to take up ballet instead of accepting his football scholarship to Notre Dame because he doesn't want to end up like his father—a boring, empty-headed, sports fanatic.

G. Tell your macho sports-aholic that you read in the *National Tattler* that two of his favorite sports legends were photographed in bed together in a sleazy hotel!

H. Make sure to hide, in a safe place, all of last year's *TV Guides*. Take the cover off the current *TV Guide* and staple it onto the *TV Guide* from last year at the same time. It will be fun to see him searching the tube for sporting events that don't exist!

10. SELECT AN ANTI-SPORTS SELF-HELP GROUP

When trying to deal with the irrational and compulsive sports fanatic, you may decide that it's time to join a self-help group to see you through these trying times. I have listed a few groups that have helped sports widows nationwide—I'm sure one of these will be able to help you contend with your unfortunate sub-station in life.

W.A.S.T.E.—WOMEN AGAINST SPORTS TELEVISION ENJOYMENT

This organization consists of a coalition of sports widows who take special lobbying field trips to major TV studios to protest the amount of sports on television. Call 555–FEUD for more info.

L.O.A.F.—LEAGUE TO OVERCOME ADDICTION TO FOOTBALL

This group deals with football as the root of all evil. Sports widows are encouraged to physically act out all their aggressions on life-size football dummies—no holds barred. You can yell at them and even kick them where they deserve it (right between the legs) for therapy. Call 555–HURT for more info.

B.U.M.S.—BUREAU FOR UNDERSTANDING MALE SPORTS-AHOLICS

The focus here is to look at the sports fanatic from the man's perspective. Women in this group dress, talk, burp, fart, bet and lounge around like their sleazeball male counterparts in a family room-type setting. Call 555–SLOB for more info.

C.L.O.D.S.—COALITION FOR LADIES OVER–DOSING ON SPORTS

This group of sports widows pay monthly dues into a fund that is used for special group outings. Favorites include singles bars, male stripper clubs like Chippendales, and crashing bachelor parties! Call 555–EVEN for more info.

M.A.N.I.C.—MOTHERS AGAINST NUBILE, INDECENT CHEERLEADERS

This special club of mothers, of all ages, meets once a month to continue an anti-cheerleading campaign for the sake of their impressionable, brainwashed sons who refuse to get married until they meet "the perfect, large breasted, bouncing cheerleader-type." Call 555–PIGS for more info.

S.L.O.T.H.—SPORTS LOSERS ORGANIZATION FOR THWARTED HOUSEWIVES

This association deals specifically with housewives who have to put up with genius husbands who constantly gamble and lose. This group offers creative solutions and special demonstrations on how to curb his gambling habits through such things as acupuncture (with the most effective area being in the groin region) and hypnosis. Call 555–PUTZ for more info.

After years of experience I have come to one conclusion: you cannot believe a word these lying boneheads say when it comes to sports! Below is a sample list of things they may tell you and next to it is what they really mean!

WHEN A SPORTS FANATIC SAYS ... HE REALLY MEANS

He Says:

"There's only three minutes left in the game."

He Means:

Official clock time is three minutes which translates into three hours of time-outs, foul shots, strategy sessions,

96

sportscaster analysis, beer and car commercials and cheer-leaders shaking their assets!

He Says:

"I'll do it during half-time."

He Means:

You can bet your sweet ass it won't get done. Notice he did not specify which half-time! Since there are many games on at the same time, and the last game ends after midnight, you might as well hire a handyman to do whatever is supposed to get done. You should make sure he's cute.

(See section on Mope Around the Dope Syndrome!)

He Says:

"I'm calling my mom to see how she is."

He Means:

I'm calling Louie to get a line on the game. It's a dead giveaway if he's whispering, or says things like "spread," "nickel," "dime," etc. You should know something's up because your guy doesn't even call his mom on Mother's Day!

He Says:

"I'm in good shape, I won't get hurt playing."

He Means:

You should check to make sure we made the last insurance payment. A 35-year-old body and a 15-year-old mind equals a one-week-stay in the hospital and three weeks of missed work.

He Says:

"I promise sports won't get in the way of our relationship."

He Means:

"I promise our relationship won't get in the way of my sports." The "big guy" will see you during the All Star Break. That's in early July, in case you want to make any big plans. As for the above-mentioned promise, notice that you can't spell r e l a t i o n s h i p s without the word sports!

He Says:

"I would never force my son into sports."

He Means:

If he wants to be a pansy, that's his business. Just don't expect me to give him money for silly things like college. Maybe he can get a job locally, as a waitress or a hair-dresser.

He Says:

"Here's a gift for you, sweetheart, some see-through shower curtains—they're the latest craze."

He Means:

He'll be able to watch TV in the bathroom while taking a shower! Don't ever fall for those phony gifts of his! Beware of all VCRs, radios, special dinners at the sports bar, athletic equipment, Watchmen and Walkmen! These are all gifts from him to him

He Says:

"I can live without sports."

He Means:

Yeah, and I don't need air either! Notice he doesn't specify for how long! Another key word here is "can"— I can live without a lot of things, but will I? My husband was late for our wedding ceremony because the Lakers went into overtime!

Revenge of the Sports Widows

He Says:

"I'm only betting on this game because the bookie owes me money."

He Means:

I'm slightly in the "hole," and I need a winner. Otherwise, we might be visited by three men you've recently seen on America's Most Wanted.

He Says:

"I love you more than anything in this world!"

He Means:

Except the Super Bowl (and the World Series, and the NBA playoffs)!

He Says:

"Just for you, honey, I won't watch sports all day!"

He Means:

There are no sports on TV today!

He Says:

"I'm not a true sports fanatic."

He Means:

He knows one guy who's even a worse ass than he is!!!!!

100

GOING FOR THE JOCK-ULAR VEIN

ROLE MODELS FOR YOUR CHILDREN

I f things worked out okay in the sex department, you may have been lucky enough to get pregnant! But once your impressionable youngsters start following in their father's footsteps you should know what kind of sports role models they will have to look up to:

Mike Tyson—Now, here's a real good role model—if you want your son to be a CONVICT! He has a dozen women alleging he raped them—now that's real macho. I also heard that he was always jealous of his ex's (Robin Givens) TV sitcom *Head of the Class.*" I guess it's ironic that his financial advisor is setting up a new sitcom for him to star in — it's going to be called *Bled of the Cash!*

Frank Gifford—A once-great running back who has turned into a real wimp. I mean, how many men would stand for their wife (Kathy Lee) telling millions of people each day the boring details of their intimate lives? I mean, who really cares that she served him lamb chops in bed the night before? (No wonder they're doing "Slimfast" commercials together!) Mr. King-of-*Monday Night Football* better get home before Kathy Lee starts to serve Regis breakfast in bed!

Mark Gastineau—His ex-wife can be seen on every talk show telling America what a sleaze and a jerk he is. Wow, I bet she didn't have a clue before they got married. I'm sure she married him for his brains, not his bank account! His one redeeming quality is the fact that he left football for a woman (Brigette Nilson)! Mark's recently been voted, "Most Likely to Take a Life" by his peers. This guy's a throwback to the Dinosaur era.

Jim Palmer—Here is a famous baseball player who is known more for the bulge in his britches than for his pitches! Talk about a Fruit of the Loom! This guy's been running around in underwear on TV for so many years that your son may think that being an exhibitionist is part of the game. Some kids may feel inferior when they try to compare themselves to him— remember kids, this is television where all objects on the screen appear larger than they are. Where do you think they got the expression "stocking stuffer" from?

Tommy Lasorda—I think the American people should be very proud of him for losing so much weight on "Slim Fast." Or it's good to know you can eat and drink like a pig and then go on a liquid diet that you'll have to stay on the rest of your life — unless you want to end up like Oprah! I think another reason Tommy has lost so much weight is because he's always got his foot in his mouth — there's no room for anything else!

Pete Rose—Odds are 10 –1 against this ball player making it into the Baseball Hall of Fame. His gambling habits became apparent when, as manager, he allegedly intentionally walked someone with the bases loaded. Nicknamed, "Charlie Hustle." I think you and I are the ones that got hustled.

George Steinbrenner—This Yankees owner, managed to make Donald Trump look modest. It has been said that Saddam Hussein looked into a mirror and said "Mirror, mirror on the wall, who is the meanest tyrant of them all?" He turned around in a rage and asked his aide, "Who is this Steinbrenner?"

Joe DiMaggio—"Where have you gone, Joe DiMaggio?" The Nation has turned their lonely eyes to watching him prostitute himself while doing those incredibly stupid Mr. Coffee commercials. Being married to Marilyn Monroe took a lot out of him. I guess after a 56-game hitting streak, and after shacking up with Marilyn, there's not much you can do for an encore.

John McEnroe—Now here is a great, well composed, poised example for a child to fashion his life after! A great tennis player, who takes losing really well, by throwing his racket on the ground, blaming all who are around him, stamping his feet and screaming expletives at everyone in sight. His punishment for this behavior is being paid millions of dollars per year! Married to Tatum O'Neil (the mature one), this guy is an embarrassment to America and the entire free world. I would like to see him play under George Steinbrenner—their first argument would register 6.3 on the Richter scale!

Billy Martin—Here was a great man for a child to look up to! A foul-mouthed, heavy drinker (not to mention lousy stunt driver!) who couldn't hold a steady job. He is sure to be immortalized in the Baseball Hall of

Shame! A charter member of AAA (Alcoholic Athletes Anonymous), Billy was loved by the fans almost as much as the umpires! It's too bad he never became an announcer. I would've loved my kids to hear him slur, "Ssshhhtrike One!"

Just to prove how great a sports hero Billy Martin was, I would like to show you a sampling of some of the jokes that have been circulating about him!

BILLY MARTIN JOKES

What's Billy doing now?

He's managing the Angels!

Did you hear that Billy Martin was on the radio?

... and the steering wheel and the dashboard and the windshield ...

What were Billy Martin's last words?

"'You idiot,' I said, 'Bud Lite, not take a right!'"

What's the last thing Billy Martin did?

He slid into home!

Why was Billy Martin cremated?

He wanted to be fired one more time!

How was Billy Martin buried?

The umpires kicked dirt all over his casket!

When you are involved with a sports fanatic you can be sure that, because of his sports infatuation, he'll be seriously deficient in the love-making department. Below are some tried and true expressions you can use to remedy this age-old problem!

LOVE LANGUAGE

Slam Dunk—You know ... what he usually does in bed!

Hole in One—No explanation needed.

Grand Slam—For that rare time when he does it right— while fantasizing about his favorite cheerleaders!

Sack—Where you'll hopefully end up, with someone other than your sports fanatic man.

Foul Ball—When he's a little off base. (Not to be confused with jock itch!)

Hit and Run—His usual *modus operandi* in bed.

Split Fingered Fastball—Don't knock it until you've tried it. (oohh!)

Behind the Back Dribble—Most men and dogs' favorite.

Illegal Use of Hands—Something most sports widows pray for.

Pick and Roll—"Pick the Lock," then roll over and go to sleep.

Fly Out—Just put it back in.

Touchdown—Touch anywhere.

Pinch Hitter—A little kinky.

The Long Bomb—The grand finale.

The Down and Out—Try again please.

Up the Middle—The old, conventional stand-by.

108

The Flea-Flicker—One of the pets is involved.

The Face Off—Removing the make-up.

Slashing—Fingernails are too long.

In the Rough—How you should sleep.

Sand Trap—Love on the beach.

Interception—Birth control.

Three-Pointer—One less than "all fours."

Assist—Guidance needed.

Tie Score—Simultaneous orgasms.

Extra Innings—Taking awhile—please concentrate.

The National Anthem—Foreplay.

Blocked Shot—Diaphragm.

Win, Place and Show—Win his heart, go to his place and show him a good time!

MOVIE REVIEWS

Below is a listing of movies that have sport themes. These are the rare movies that you both can enjoy watching together. Wouldn't that be a nice change!

The Longest Yard: Great flick! Lots of hunks. You get a quick look at a young, Burt Reynolds' buns! Oh, yeah, I think there's some football in it too!

Brian's Song: Don't look for the album! It's about a dying football player—oh, what a shame!

North Dallas Forty: Another great movie—Nick Nolte naked in a whirlpool! Shows that football players are absolutely nuts, not to mention lowlifes (our boyfriends and husbands' role models!)

Field Of Dreams: As if we didn't have enough movies about baseball players, now we need "dead" ones coming back as ghosts. But, it's worth is just for the sake of Kevin Costner!

The Natural: Robert Redford, 'nuff said? A dream movie.

Eight Men Out: This is not about a night in the Hamptons— it's about the World Series that was fixed! I didn't even know it was broken!

Major League: Tom Berenger another hunk! Also, Charlie Sheen, if you're into macho studs! Oh, yeah, there's a plot, too.

Bull Durham: Not a brand of tobacco, but a baseball player, Kevin Costner, before he was "untouchable" by dancing with wolves!"

Slapshot: Gorgeous Paul Newman as a hockey goon! Almost makes hockey likable!

Days Of Thunder: After watching Tom Cruise in this, you'll have many nights of thunder!

Rocky I: Barely watchable. Fortunately, you can hardly understand Stallone!

Rocky II: Barely watchable. Fortunately, you can hardly understand Stallone!

Rocky III: Barely watchable. Fortunately, you can hardly understand Stallone!

Rocky IV: Barely watchable. Fortunately, you can hardly understand Stallone!

Rocky V: Barely watchable. Fortunately, you can hardly understand Stallone!

Rocky X: Barely watchable. Fortunately, you can hardly understand Stallone!

WHEEL OF MISFORTUNE

Analysis of the Dispersal of a Sports Fanatics Income
* VIG: Bookie's 10% cut (slightly more than wive's)

A
CHILLING
CONCLUSION

o now that we know the different types of sports fanatics, it's up to you to decide which path your life will take. I have touched upon some of the ways you can learn to cope with these thorns in our sides. Will you give in and let him indulge in his sports fanatical ways, or will you opt for separation or divorce?

First, let's look at the option of sticking it out and trying to survive in his world because, unfortunately no matter how hard you try, sports will continue to endure for him and be the basis of his weak existence. One way you can do this is to completely become a sports fanatic's "Dream Girl." I don't advocate this but below I've listed what I call the three A's to becoming his perfect partner.

HOW TO BECOME THE SPORTS FANATIC'S "DREAM GIRL"

ATTITUDE

This is the most important thing you must change. Don't even think for one second that your life is very boring and meaningless with a man who doesn't even acknowledge your existence. Try listening to headphones while you are sleeping that keep repeating the phrase "Sports is synonymous with sex" over and over again. This will help you to watch sporting events on TV, or worse yet, in person from a new perspective. When you are watching a football game for instance, don't think of it as a bunch of infantile men running up and down the field trying to catch a ball that's shaped like a suppository. Instead look really hard at each man as a sexual object who is in the prime of his life physically and sexually and when his cute little bod is prancing down the sidelines, try to fantasize what you could do to this guy if you ever got

your hands on him. I don't know about you but I know a "tight end" when I see one. Try to get excited when your sports fanatic shows excitement over certain plays. Observe which cheerleaders really turn him on and at the right moment allow him to fantasize he's with her. Watch him get hot and try to use this to your advantage. When he starts squirming and yelling and screaming make sure you match him thrust for thrust.

Once he begins to trust that you have seen the light and really enjoy sports he might let down his guard and start to respect you more. You will suddenly be able to influence him again, just like it was when you first met and you called the shots. Try to become more cheerleaderish—say things like "golly" and "gee whiz" while naively giggling as you bounce up and down on his lap. If you're young enough try a few cartwheels during half time, make sure to wear your sheer lacy bikini underwear.

APPEARANCE

There are only two ways you can dress up to please a sports fanatic. The first way, mentioned previously, is to dress up as his favorite cheerleader. However, if you're not in good shape this could turn out to be a turn-off. The other way to dress, believe-it-or-not, would be like one of his buddies. Borrow some of his old football jerseys and make sure that you strategically place a few rips and holes where he can get a glimpse of those seldom-seen private parts. The subliminal message may eventually sink in. Instead of eyeshadow, go out in the backyard and get a little dirt from your garden to smear under your eyes—this really gets them horny.

APTITUDE

Unfortunately, if you want to become his dream girl you must learn a few of the basic rules of his sport (or sports) of choice. Any book store will sell the basic rule books that you can study. The advantage to this is, instead of verbal communication, which has rarely worked in the past, you can now use hand signals to get his attention. For instance you can try a few of these:

SIGNAL:

WHAT IT MEANS:

Your water broke and you need a ride to the hospital.

SIGNAL:

WHAT IT MEANS:

Your mother decided not to come over after all, or your pregnancy test came back negative.

SIGNAL:

WHAT IT MEANS:

You need some money to go shopping.

SIGNAL:

WHAT IT MEANS:

You're sick of his stupid sports addiction.

SIGNAL:

WHAT IT MEANS:

You're in the mood for love.

SPORTS QUIZ

(SUPER EASY)

It is quite possible that you may know more about sports than you realize. After years and years of being subjected to a male-dominated, sports-filled world, something was bound to be absorbed in our pretty little female brains. Try to take the following quiz, and if you can come up with a few correct answers, you may be able to communicate with your sports fanatic on a new level—his (a much lower level, of course).

1. Which one is not a sports team?

    A.) Mets
    B.) Nets
    C.) Sets
    D.) Yets

Revenge of the Sports Widows

2. Who is the baseball team owner?

   A.) Joel Steinberg
   B.) Andrew Stein
   C.) Gertrude Stein
   D.) George Steinbrenner

3. Who is not a famous gambler?

   A.) Jimmy the Greek
   B.) Pete Axthelm
   C.) Pete Rose
   D.) Bradford Marsalis

4. What is the most popular food at a ballpark?

   A.) Filet Mignon
   B.) Mexican combination platter
   C.) Sushi
   D.) Ice cold franks and rock-hard pretzels

5. Which topic is a sports fanatic least likely to discuss?

   A.) George Brett's average
   B.) Mookie Wilson's salary
   C.) Don Mattingly's arbitration
   D.) Bill Clinton's budget proposals.

6. What accessory is not important to a sports fanatic while watching a game?

   A.) Remote control
   B.) Sports section of the newspaper
   C.) Beer and nuts
   D.) A wife

7. Which of these is not a basketball term?

   A.) Slam dunk
   B.) Offensive foul
   C.) Pick and roll
   D.) Deviated septum

8. Who makes under three million dollars per year?

   A.) Michael Jordan
   B.) Wayne Gretzky
   C.) Jose Canseco
   D.) Dan Quayle

9. Who is not a famous sportscaster?

   A.) Frank Gifford
   B.) Howard Cosell
   C.) Phyllis George
   D.) George Phyllis

10. Which is the least important event to a sports fanatic?

    A.) Super Bowl
    B.) World Series
    C.) Stanley Cup playoffs
    D.) War in the Middle East

11. Which is not a famous-brand sneaker?

    A.) Addidas
    B.) Nike
    C.) Puma
    D.) Hush Puppies

12. Who has not been suspended for drugs?

    A.) Dwight Gooden
    B.) Dexter Manley
    C.) Sugar Ray Richardson
    D.) Mayor Barry

13. Which is not a gambling term?

    A.) "Give me the Knicks ten times"
    B.) "I'll take the points for a nickel"
    C.) "Give me the over/under on reverse"
    D.) "Honey, is the pizza ready?"

14. Which newspaper has the best sports coverage?

    A.) *Sporting News*
    B.) *The Daily News*
    C.) *USA Today*
    D.) *The Wall Street Journal*

15. Where is it illegal to bet on sports?

    A.) Las Vegas
    B.) Atlantic City
    C.) The office
    D.) Pete Rose's house

16. Which is the least strenuous sport?

    A.) Baseball
    B.) Basketball
    C.) Boxing
    D.) Backgammon

17. Who is the meanest and ugliest man in professional boxing?

    A.) Mike Tyson

B.) George Foreman

C.) Buster Douglas

D.) Bob Saget

18. What should you never do while a sports fanatic is watching a game?

A.) Serve beer and pretzels

B.) Root for his team with him

C.) Give him a back massage

D.) Stand in front of the TV and show him your new clothes

19. Which of these is not a sport?

A.) Lacrosse

B.) Fencing

C.) Slaloming

D.) Crocheting

20. What is the best way to score tickets for a hard-to-get sporting event?

A.) Using a ticket broker

B.) Buying them at the window

C.) Buying them from a scalper

D.) Forgetting about it—it's on cable!

21. When entering an office football pool, what is the best way to make your pick?

A.) Use your sports acumen

B.) Read the sports analyst columns

C.) Flip a coin

D.) Ask the most handsome hunk for help

22. Who is known for giving the most vicious beating?

    A.) Mike Tyson
    B.) George Foreman
    C.) Mohammed Ali
    D.) The L.A.P.D.

23. What is the most important factor in an athlete's life?

    A.) Pure motivation
    B.) Pure drive
    C.) Pure ambition
    D.) Pure Colombian cocaine

24. Why do gamblers like to bet on college football games more than the pros?

    A.) It's more exciting
    B.) It's more unpredictable
    C.) It's more fun watching fresh talent
    D.) It's easier to fix

25. When is it most likely that there will be no sports on TV?

    A.) In the summer
    B.) In the winter
    C.) On holidays
    D.) October 27 between 10:00 A.M. and 12:20 P.M.

26. Which is the most commonly heard bowling expression?

    A.) Oh, no—a split!
    B.) C'mon I need a strike!
    C.) A perfect frame!
    D.) Aaarggh! I dropped the ball on my ingrown toe nail!

27. Who is the most important person in an athlete's life?

    A.) His manager
    B.) His mom
    C.) His fans
    D.) His agent

28. Which is not a baseball statistic?

    A.) Batting average
    B.) Slugging percentage
    C.) Number of RBI's
    D.) Number of times arrested

29. Who is the least popular public figure?

    A.) Yassir Arafat
    B.) Moammar Khaddafy
    C.) Saddam Hussein
    D.) George Steinbrenner

30. What foods should you never serve to a sports fanatic?

    A.) Beer and nuts
    B.) Pepperoni pizza
    C.) Pretzels
    D.) Cottage cheese and a salad with alfalfa sprouts

EXTRA INNINGS
(OR SUDDEN DEATH)

One final alternative to end sports widowhood is either separation or divorce. I feel this is a really drastic step for the simple reason that three out of every four males on this planet are sports fanatics, and 3.5 out of every four sports widows put up with them. Unless you would consider lesbianism, the odds will be against you finding the perfect male specimen.

Please review this book and try to cope. Hopefully the knowledge you've gained by delving into the deviant personality of the sports fanatic will help. Cheer up, there's always next season.